Disney FAVORITES

FOR OCARINA

Disney characters and artwork © Disney

ISBN 978-1-70517-437-1

Visit Hal Leonard Online at
www.halleonard.com

World headquarters, contact:
Hal Leonard
7777 West Bluemound Road
Milwaukee, WI 53213
Email: info@halleonard.com

In Europe, contact:
Hal Leonard Europe Limited
42 Wigmore Street
Marylebone, London, W1U 2RN
Email: info@halleonardeurope.com

In Australia, contact:
Hal Leonard Australia Pty. Ltd.
4 Lentara Court
Cheltenham, Victoria, 3192 Australia
Email: info@halleonard.com.au

Table of Contents

ALMOST THERE
from THE PRINCESS AND THE FROG

OCARINA

Music and Lyrics by
RANDY NEWMAN

THE BALLAD OF THE LONESOME COWBOY

from TOY STORY 4

OCARINA

Music and Lyrics by
RANDY NEWMAN

rit.   a tempo

BEAUTY AND THE BEAST

from BEAUTY AND THE BEAST

OCARINA

Music by ALAN MENKEN
Lyrics by HOWARD ASHMAN

BELLA NOTTE
from LADY AND THE TRAMP

OCARINA

Words and Music by PEGGY LEE
and SONNY BURKE

CIRCLE OF LIFE
from THE LION KING

OCARINA

Music by ELTON JOHN
Lyrics by TIM RICE

CRUELLA DE VIL

from 101 DALMATIANS

Words and Music by
MEL LEVEN

OCARINA

A DREAM IS A WISH YOUR HEART MAKES

from CINDERELLA

OCARINA

Music by MACK DAVID and AL HOFFMAN
Lyrics by JERRY LIVINGSTON

DOS ORUGUITAS
from ENCANTO

OCARINA

Music and Lyrics by
LIN-MANUEL MIRANDA

FRIEND LIKE ME

from ALADDIN

OCARINA

Music by ALAN MENKEN
Lyrics by HOWARD ASHMAN

GOD HELP THE OUTCASTS

from THE HUNCHBACK OF NOTRE DAME

OCARINA

Music by ALAN MENKEN
Lyrics by STEPHEN SCHWARTZ

IF I DIDN'T HAVE YOU

from MONSTERS, INC.

OCARINA

Music and Lyrics by
RANDY NEWMAN

IF I NEVER KNEW YOU

(End Title)

from POCAHONTAS

Music by ALAN MENKEN
Lyrics by STEPHEN SCHWARTZ

OCARINA

LEAD THE WAY
from RAYA AND THE LAST DRAGON

OCARINA

Music and Lyrics by
JHENÉ AIKO

INTO THE UNKNOWN
from FROZEN 2

OCARINA

Music and Lyrics by KRISTEN ANDERSON-LOPEZ
and ROBERT LOPEZ

Mysteriously, in 2

LET IT GO
from FROZEN

OCARINA

Music and Lyrics by KRISTEN ANDERSON-LOPEZ
and ROBERT LOPEZ

Slowly, in 2

LOVE IS AN OPEN DOOR

from FROZEN

OCARINA

Music and Lyrics by KRISTEN ANDERSON-LOPEZ
and ROBERT LOPEZ

THE PLACE WHERE LOST THINGS GO

from MARY POPPINS RETURNS

Music by MARC SHAIMAN
Lyrics by SCOTT WITTMAN and MARC SHAIMAN

OCARINA

PART OF YOUR WORLD

from THE LITTLE MERMAID

OCARINA

Music by ALAN MENKEN
Lyrics by HOWARD ASHMAN

REFLECTION

from MULAN

OCARINA

Music by MATTHEW WILDER
Lyrics by DAVID ZIPPEL

REMEMBER ME
(Ernesto de la Cruz)
from COCO

OCARINA

Music and Lyrics by KRISTEN ANDERSON-LOPEZ
and ROBERT LOPEZ

SOMEDAY

from THE HUNCHBACK OF NOTRE DAME

Music by ALAN MENKEN
Lyrics by STEPHEN SCHWARTZ

OCARINA

SHOW YOURSELF

from FROZEN 2

OCARINA

Music and Lyrics by KRISTEN ANDERSON-LOPEZ
and ROBERT LOPEZ

SO CLOSE
from ENCHANTED

OCARINA

Music by ALAN MENKEN
Lyrics by STEPHEN SCHWARTZ

Moderately slow, in 4

Slowly, freely

SPEECHLESS
from ALADDIN

OCARINA

Music by ALAN MENKEN
Lyrics by BENJ PASEK
and JUSTIN PAUL

Half-time feel

SURFACE PRESSURE

from ENCANTO

OCARINA

Music and Lyrics by
LIN-MANUEL MIRANDA

UN POCO LOCO

from COCO

OCARINA

Music by GERMAINE FRANCO
Lyrics by ADRIAN MOLINA

Moderately, in 2, with a bounce

WHEN SHE LOVED ME

from TOY STORY 2

OCARINA

Music and Lyrics by
RANDY NEWMAN

Tenderly, very freely

WE DON'T TALK ABOUT BRUNO
from ENCANTO

OCARINA

Music and Lyrics by
LIN-MANUEL MIRANDA

Moderate Cha-Cha

45

YOU'LL BE IN MY HEART

(Pop Version)*
from TARZAN®

Ocarina

Words and Music by
PHIL COLLINS

WHEN WILL MY LIFE BEGIN?

from TANGLED

Music by ALAN MENKEN
Lyrics by GLENN SLATER

OCARINA